DK READERS

STAR WARS REBELS

™

MEET THE REBELS

Written by Sadie Smith

DK LONDON

Senior Editor Sadie Smith
Pre-Production Producer Siu Yin Chan
Producer David Appleyard
Managing Editor Laura Gilbert
Managing Art Editor Maxine Pedliham
Art Director Lisa Lanzarini
Publisher Julie Ferris
Publishing Director Simon Beecroft

DK DELHI

Editor Rahul Ganguly
Art Editor Suzena Sengupta
Managing Editor Chitra Subramanyam
Managing Art Editor Neha Ahuja
Pre-Production Manager Sunil Sharma
DTP Designers Rajdeep Singh, Umesh Singh Rawat

For Lucasfilm

Executive Editor Jonathan W. Rinzler
Art Director Troy Alders
Keeper of the Holocron Leland Chee
Director of Publishing Carol Roeder

Reading Consultant
Linda Gambrell, PhD.

First American Edition, 2014

15 16 10 9 8 7 6 5
008–266537–Aug/14

Published in the United States by DK Publishing
345 Hudson Street, New York, New York 10014

© & TM 2015 LUCASFILM LTD

Published in Great Britain by Dorling Kindersley Limited

A catalog record for this book is available from the Library of Congress.

ISBN: 978-1-4654-2268-2 (Hardback)
ISBN: 978-1-4654-2269-9 (Paperback)

Color Reproduction by Alta Image Ltd, UK
Printed and bound in the U.S.A. by Lake Book Manufacturing, Inc.

www.starwars.com
www.dk.com

A WORLD OF IDEAS:
SEE ALL THERE IS TO KNOW

Contents

Rebellion on Lothal

Meet the rebels.
Their names are
Sabine, Ezra, Kanan,
Hera, Zeb, and Chopper.
They live on a planet
called Lothal.

Lothal is under the rule
of an evil Empire.
The rebels are fighting
against the Empire
and its soldiers.

Ezra Bridger

This is Ezra.

He is just 14 years old,
but he is brave and smart.
Ezra is also a lot of fun!
He likes to play tricks on
and steal helmets from
the Emperor's soldiers.

A view of Lothal
Ezra lives in an old, empty
tower on Lothal. From there,
he can see factories of the
Empire blow out black smoke.

Messy hair

Belt for tools

Special Power

Ezra is special.

Sometimes, he can see

things a few seconds

before they happen.

Useful backpack

This is because Ezra is

in touch with a special power

called the Force.

Ezra does not understand

how to use this power.

Maybe someone

can teach him...

Knee protection

Kanan Jarrus

Kanan is a Jedi.
The Jedi are trained
to fight for good.
Their job is to protect
the galaxy from evil.
The Emperor does
not like the Jedi,
so Kanan has to keep
his Jedi skills secret.

Shoulder armor

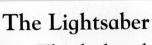

The Lightsaber

The lightsaber
is the favorite
weapon of the
Jedi. It is like a
sword, but its blade is
made of pure energy.

Garazeb "Zeb" Orrelios

The rebel Zeb is
very big and strong.
He is a Lasat from
the planet Lasan.
Zeb likes nothing better
than to fight stormtroopers.
The stormtroopers are
soldiers in the army of
the evil Emperor.

Stormtroopers
Some of the stormtroopers
are people from Lothal.
The evil Empire has made
these people fight for them.

Hera Syndulla

Hera is a Twi'lek from
a planet called Ryloth.
This clever rebel leads
the group with Kanan.
She plans all their missions.
Hera owns a spaceship
called the *Ghost*.
She is a great pilot.

The *Ghost*
The *Ghost* is a medium-
sized spaceship. It is
also the rebels' home.

Sabine Wren

Colorful Sabine
is an artist from the
planet Mandalore.
She is usually covered
in paint!
Sabine takes care of the
weapons of the rebels.
She is also good at
blowing things up.

C1-10P "Chopper"

Chopper is a type of robot
called an astromech droid.
He helps the rebels
by repairing their spaceship.
Chopper speaks a
special robot language.
Only Hera and Sabine
can understand him.

Chopper and Ezra

Most of the rebels think
Chopper is too grumpy.
They do not even try to
be friends with him.
However, Ezra loves
playing tricks on Chopper.
The little droid likes to
play tricks on Ezra, too!

Aresko and Grint

Aresko and Grint are
bad guys who work
for the evil Empire.
Aresko is pale and thin.
He thinks he is
very smart—but he is not!
Grint is tall and bulky.
He is just a big bully.

Agent Kallus

Agent Kallus works for
the Empire's secret police.
This villain tracks people
who are plotting against
the Emperor.

Agent Kallus is smart
and dangerous.
Watch out, rebels!

The Inquisitor

This scary villain carries
a powerful lightsaber
with two blades!
The Inquisitor has
been sent to Lothal
by Agent Kallus.
His job is to hunt
for Jedi who may be
hiding on the planet.

*Double-bladed
lightsaber*

Stormtrooper

Quiz

1. Which planet do the rebels live on?

2. What is Ezra's special power called?

3. What is the favorite weapon of the Jedi?

4. Who does the *Ghost* spaceship belong to?

5. What does Kanan have to keep secret?

6. Which planet is Sabine from?

7. Who does Zeb like to fight?

8. What type of robot is Chopper?

9. Who does Agent Kallus work for?

10. What weapon does the Inquisitor use?

Answers on page 31

Glossary

Droid
A type of robot. Chopper is a droid.

Emperor
Somebody who rules over
a group of nations

Jedi
A warrior who fights
for good

Lightsaber
A swordlike weapon
with a blade
of pure energy

Pilot
A person who flies
a spacecraft

Index

Answers to the quiz on pages 28 and 29:
1. Lothal 2. The Force 3. A lightsaber 4. Hera
5. His Jedi skills 6. Mandalore 7. Stormtroopers
8. Astromech droid 9. The secret police
10. A lightsaber with two blades

Here are some other DK Readers you might enjoy.

Level 2

Pirate Attack!
Join Captain Blackbeard and his pirate crew
for an action-packed adventure on the high seas.

Deadly Dinosaurs
Roar! Thud! Meet Roxy, Sid, Deano, and Sonia,
the museum dinosaurs that come alive at night.

LEGO® Legends of Chima™: Tribes of Chima
Enter the mysterious land of Chima™ and discover
the amazing animal tribes who live there.

Level 3

Battle at the Castle
Through the letters of a squire to his sister, discover life
in a medieval castle during peacetime and war.

African Adventures
Experience the trip of a lifetime on an African safari
as recorded in Katie's diary. Share her excitement
when seeing wild animals up close.

LEGO® Legends of Chima™: Heroes' Quest
Who are the mysterious Legend Beasts?
Join the heroes of Chima™ on their quest
to find these mythical creatures.